Thanks to Dr. Petra Sierwald,
The Field Museum of Natural History,
Chicago, IL

For Emily
— F.R.

For Emily
— J.D.Z.

Text copyright © 1996 by Fay Robinson.
Illustrations copyright © 1996 by Jean Day Zallinger.
All rights reserved. Published by Scholastic Inc.
Printed in the U.S.A.
ISBN 0-590-06682-X
HELLO READER!, CARTWHEEL BOOKS and the CARTWHEEL BOOKS logo are registered
trademarks of Scholastic Inc.

5 6 7 8 9 10   23   03 02 01 00 99 98

Mighty Spiders!

by Fay Robinson
Illustrated by Jean Day Zallinger

Hello Science Reader!

SCHOLASTIC INC. Cartwheel ·B·O·O·K·S· ®
New York Toronto London Auckland Sydney

Spiders up.

Spiders down.

Mighty spiders all around!

Eight strong legs.
Tough, hard skin.

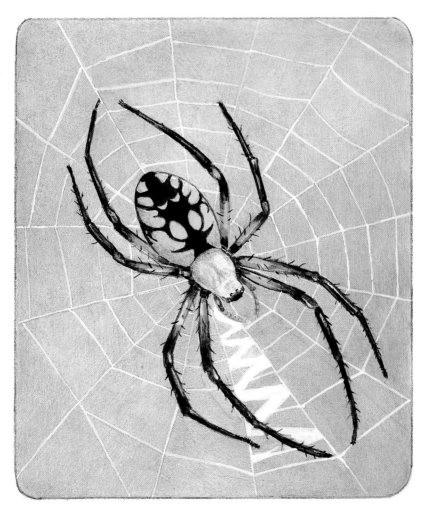

Silky webs to scurry in.

Spiders anywhere you please —

on the ground

and high in trees.

Under water,

sand,

and stone.

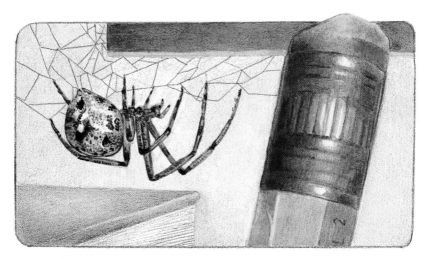

Spiders creeping in your home.

Green and yellow.

Flashy pink.

White like snowflakes.

Black like ink.

Spider stripes

and starry thorns.

Spider hearts

and spider horns.

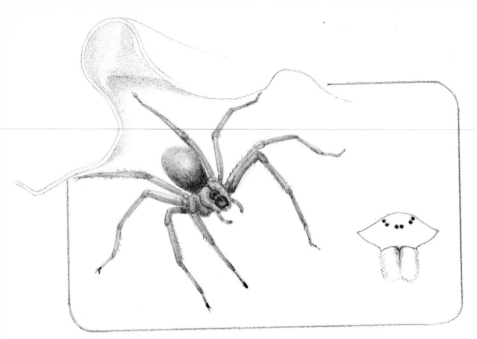

Six eyes,

eight eyes,
large and small.

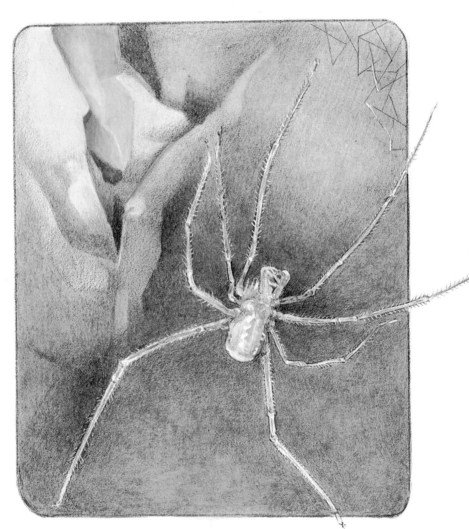

Spiders with no eyes at all.

Spiders small as grains of sand.

Spiders bigger than your hand.

Spiders spin a silky thread —
a thread that sometimes
makes a web.

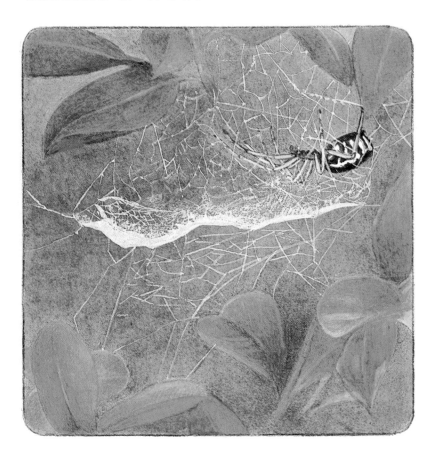

Webs in tangles.

Webs in wheels.

Webs for catching

spider meals —

a moth, a wasp,
a juicy fly.

Any bug that wanders by.

Other spiders stalk and hunt,
doing mighty spider stunts.

Spiders hiding,

spiders creeping,

spiders diving,

spiders leaping.

Snatching insects,

birds, or frogs,

lizards, fish,
or pollywogs.

Mothers make a silk cocoon.
Tiny eggs inside hatch soon.

Babies crawling from their sac.

Babies riding piggyback.

Babies shedding too-small skin.

Babies blowing in the wind.

Spiders up and spiders down.
Mighty spiders all around!

Cover:
Black Widow

Page 4:
American House
Spider

Page 5:
American House
Spider

Page 6:
Black and Yellow
Garden Spider

Page 7:
Burrowing Wolf Spider

Page 7:
Pink-toed Tarantula

Page 8:
European Water Spider

Page 8:
Dancing White Lady

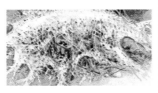

Page 9:
Mediterranean Tent
Builder

Page 9:
American House Spider

Page 10:
Green Huntsman Spider

Page 10:
Heather Spider

Page 11:
White Crab Spider

Page 11:
Black Widow

Page 12:
Zebra Spider

Page 14:
Wolf Spider

Page 19:
Marbled Spider

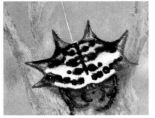

Page 12:
Spiny-backed Spider

Page 15:
Cave Spider

Page 20:
Barn Spider

Page 13:
Bolas Spider

Page 16:
Dwarf Spider

Page 21:
Trapdoor Spider

Page 13:
Spiny-backed Spider

Page 17:
Red-legged Tarantula

Page 22:
Green Lynx Spider

Page 14:
Brown Recluse Spider

Page 18:
Bowl and Doily Spider

Page 22:
European Water Spider

Page 23:
Jumping Spider

Page 24:
Jumping Spider

Page 24:
Bird-eating Spider

Page 25:
Fishing Spider

Page 26:
Nursery Web Spider

Page 26:
Black Widow Spider
with spiderlings

Page 27:
Wolf Spider with
spiderlings

Page 27:
Orb Weaver

Page 28:
Nursery Web
Spiderlings

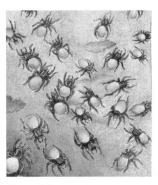

Page 29:
Monkey Spiderlings